T0112609

OVERCOMING OBSTACLES

OVERCOMING OBSTACLES

A NAVY SEAL'S GUIDE TO BEATING ADVERSITY AND FINDING SUCCESS

DON MANN
WITH KRAIG BECKER

Skyhorse Publishing

Skyhorse Publishing books may be purchased in bulk at special discounts for sales promotion, corporate gifts, fund-raising, or educational purposes. Special editions can also be created to specifications. For details, contact the Special Sales Department, Skyhorse Publishing, 307 West 36th Street, 11th Floor, New York, NY 10018 or info@skyhorsepublishing.com.

Skyhorse® and Skyhorse Publishing® are registered trademarks of Skyhorse Publishing, Inc.®, a Delaware corporation.

Visit our website at www.skyhorsepublishing.com.

10 9 8 7 6 5 4 3 2

Library of Congress Cataloging-in-Publication Data is available on file.

Cover design by Brian Peterson

Print ISBN: 978-1-5107-4573-5
Ebook ISBN: 978-1-5107-4576-6

Printed in China

CONTENTS

PART I

IDENTIFYING THE OBSTACLES IN YOUR LIFE

On May 2, 2011, US Navy SEALs carried out a daring raid on a heavily-fortified compound located in Abbottabad, Pakistan, with the hope of capturing or killing the most wanted man on the planet. An anonymous tip from a Pakistani informer, followed by extensive surveillance and reconnaissance by US intelligence operatives, indicated that the fortress-like structure could very well be the hiding place of Osama bin Laden, the terrorist leader who planned the attacks on the World Trade Center and the Pentagon on September 11, 2001.

Bin Laden had gone into hiding in the years that followed the 9/11 attacks and there were very few indications of his potential whereabouts. The Al-Qaeda leader had taken great measures to stay off the grid, avoiding the use of cell phones, satellite communications devices, and internet connections, while still managing to direct his global network of terrorists using low-tech options. Despite adopting a low-profile on the global stage, he remained at the very top of the list of America's Most Wanted, with an ongoing global manhunt that was laser focused on bringing him to justice.

When the members of SEAL Team Six embarked on Operation Neptune Spear—as the mission was code named—they boarded three helicopters in Jalalabad, Afghanistan, having already been thoroughly briefed on what to expect once they arrived in Abbottabad. Intel told them that the three-story-tall compound was surrounded by a thick wall topped with razor-sharp barbwire. Furthermore, there were two security gates that would need to be breached, not to mention an unknown number of individuals—possibly even women and children—roaming around inside the building.

It was a complex and challenging undertaking to say the least, but not one that was all that unusual for the veteran SEALs who were taking part in the operation. The men who make up this highly secretive counter-terrorist group are often tasked with hostage rescues, special recon expeditions, and rapid assault operations. For them, Operation Neptune Spear was exactly what they had spent years training for, and had already lived through, at various times in the past.

When planning for the mission, the team identified a number of obstacles that could get in the way of their success, not the least of which was not knowing just how many people were inside the compound and how well armed they might be. Thanks to intelligence gathering and surveillance reports, the team did have a basic understanding of the layout of the compound itself, but no one was quite sure what the SEALs would find once they actually breached the interior of the building. Perhaps the entire place would be rigged with explosives, or maybe an impenetrable hidden bunker would be found underneath. Were there highly trained guards waiting for them inside, or would they face limited resistance instead? Was the place filled with dangerous IEDs, or were the inhabitants themselves wearing explosive devices?

In addition to all of those questions, the SEALs weren't exactly sure *who* they would find inside either. US intelligence agents had tracked a careless Al-Qaeda operative to the compound, but months of surveillance had provided no hard evidence that the group's leader was actually hidden inside. Still, there were a few clues as to who might possibly be living there. For instance, a seven-foot-tall privacy wall had been erected along a third-story balcony, making it the perfect hiding place for the six-foot, four-inch terrorist. The lack of phone and internet lines, coupled with the frequent comings and goings of a specific courier, did lend credence to the idea that a high-level Al-Qaeda operative was in residence. But without visual identification, no one could say with any level of certainty that it was indeed Osama bin Laden.

In preparation for the raid, the SEAL team trained at a secret facility built to replicate the compound in Pakistan as closely as possible. During those drills, they prepared for just about every imaginable contingency while working to become as speedy and silent as possible. The Navy's elite warriors are already incredibly efficient at their jobs, but in this case they knew that time would be of the essence, and success or failure could hinge on being precise and decisive.

In the end, all of their training, planning, and preparation would prove essential to the successful completion of the mission. Intelligence operatives estimated that the SEAL team would have approximately forty minutes to complete the operation. During that time they would have to breach the outer wall, storm the building, eliminate any hostiles, bag their high-profile target, collect as much useful intel as they could carry, and get back out again. Any longer than that and it was likely that Pakistani authorities would be alerted to the raid and could potentially respond with force. That could have been potentially disastrous for the SEAL team itself, but would also prove to be a serious PR nightmare for the US military and government. Once the smoke had cleared, however, the entire operation took just thirty-eight minutes to complete, with bin Laden himself being eliminated within the first fifteen minutes.

Operation Neptune Spear is easily the most high-profile SEAL operation that has ever been revealed to the public. It proved to be a major success not just because Osama bin Laden was eliminated at long last, but also because the SEALs came home with a treasure trove of intelligence data. The team collected numerous hard drives, laptops, USB drives, and hardcopy files that offered details on the inner workings of the Al-Qaeda organization, all without losing a single man or incurring any serious injuries.

Of course, the Navy SEALs and intelligence officers who took part in the raid are professionals whose job it is to identify and eliminate obstacles that can get in the way of the success of a mission. These individuals have gone through extensive training that allows them to identify potential challenges and find ways to overcome them. Their jobs—and often their wellbeing—depend on knowing what they'll face in the field and being prepared to take on any obstacle that comes their way. That so happens to be a skillset that can benefit non-SEALs as well, as we all face obstacles in achieving the things we want to do in our lives on a regular basis.

" It is not the mountain we conquer, but ourselves.**"**

—Sir Edmund Hillary

In the purest sense of the word, an obstacle is something that blocks our way or hinders our progress towards a destination or goal. Obviously, obstacles can come in a number of different forms and sizes, although all are impediments to our success. Large obstacles are often those that are the most difficult to overcome, while smaller ones present simpler hurdles that are usually less of a challenge to negotiate. Similarly, obstacles that are physical in nature—ones that we can see, feel, and touch—are generally less complicated to work around simply because they are easier for us to comprehend and formulate a plan to circumvent.

Conversely, some of the most challenging obstacles of all are the ones that are intangible, meaning they can't be easily seen or touched. These types of obstacles usually come from within ourselves, often in the form of self-doubt, indecision, and fear. Facing those challenges can be difficult, as it often requires a great deal of self-reflection and introspection.

Whether you're starting a new business,

designing a groundbreaking product, or just setting goals for your own personal health and fitness, you'll almost certainly face more than a few obstacles on your road to success. One of the things you'll want to do first after setting a goal for yourself is to begin to identify the obstacles you think you could encounter along the way. Sometimes those obstacles will come in the form of a direct competitor or the environment around us. Other times, it will be something more ethereal, such as a lack of time to prepare or our own fears rising up to hold us back. Either way, being able to recognize these barriers and finding a way to go over, around, or through them will be crucial to achieving whatever it is we've set out to accomplish.

The first step to overcoming any obstacle that stands in your way is identifying exactly what those obstacles actually are. At times this will be something that is fairly straightforward and easy to do, as many of the challenges we face will seem obvious at first glance. This can include things like a fellow competitor in an athletic event or the need to raise capital to start a business. And while these types of obstacles may be easy to identify, that doesn't mean that they are necessarily easy to overcome.

In order to identify the obstacles you could face when embarking on just about any endeavor, it often pays to sit down and make a list of the challenges that you anticipate along the way. For instance, when preparing to successfully run a marathon you might list such things as "finding time to train" and "creating a proper nutritional plan." On the other hand, if you're looking to get a business off the ground, the list might contain items such as "locate affordable office space" or "find investors."

The entire point of the list is to make it easier for us to assess the challenges that lie ahead in order to be better prepared to eventually deal with them. After all, you can't clear a hurdle if you don't even know that it exists. At this stage you're not necessarily trying to find ways to overcome the obstacles—that will come later—but instead you're focused on gathering knowledge and information that could help you to be better prepared for when the time comes to deal with the challenges that could potentially trip you up.

You may also find that there are plenty of obstacles that can be surprisingly difficult to identify, which in turn makes them much more challenging to plan for and find ways to overcome. Those types of road blocks often force us to be more thoughtful, requiring a higher degree of personal introspection just to identify them. Those obstacles will take the form of self-doubt, uncertainty, and indecision, which can bring a level of paralysis that keeps us from moving forward with our plans. Believe it or not, many people fail to achieve their goals simply because they can't overcome one of the biggest and most challenging obstacles of all—their own fears.

The SEALs that assaulted Osama bin Laden's compound in Pakistan easily identified the obvious obstacles including the exterior walls, security gates, and the armed personnel located inside the building. They also knew that Pakistani military and local police could cause major problems if they were alerted to the operation. Variables such as wind, temperature, and even the phase of the moon were taken into consideration and accounted for as well. Those things may seem trivial to the untrained civilian, but taking those seemingly inconsequential factors into account gave Operation Neptune Spear a greater chance of success.

What wasn't known was just how many hostiles were located inside the compound, as well as what types of weapons they had at their disposal. The exact layout of the interior of the home remained a mystery, too, as did the location of the high-value asset that they were hunting. Even with all of the sophisticated technology and modern intelligence gathering that the military had at its disposal, there was still a measure of guesswork that went into planning for the mission.

The SEALs' training and experience helped to eliminate concerns about fear and self-doubt because the men who were a part of Operation Neptune Spear had faced similar challenges in the past. Not only had they drilled countless times for the mission prior to setting out for Pakistan, they had conducted these types of raids before. This made each of them preeminently qualified to be a part of the team, which consisted of some of the most skilled and well-trained warriors on the planet.

Knowledge and experience can play a critical role in identifying obstacles, allowing us to better understand and evaluate the challenges we face at any given time. When you've encountered similar challenges in the past, the ability to spot those same kind of hurdles—and find ways to get past them—becomes much easier. Experience and familiarity can turn what was once a seemingly insurmountable obstacle into nothing more than a mole hill that becomes just a speed bump on the path to our objectives. Along the way, it can provide a nice boost to our confidence too.

Of course, the opposite can be true as well. Not properly identifying an obstacle can create a road block that may seem impossible to overcome upon first glance, especially if you've never dealt with a similar challenge before. This can end up shaking your confidence and decision-making abilities to the core, causing you to rethink your entire strategy. At those times, it is important to step back, take a breath, realistically assess the situation, and look for solutions that provide a clear path that allows us to forge ahead.

66

We may encounter many defeats but we must not be defeated."

—Maya Angelou

In the end however, dealing with the unknown is simply a part of the learning process that allows us to continue advancing towards our goals. Keep in mind that no matter how much we plan, prepare, and train, there will always be things we don't see coming. Such was the case for the two men who became the first to summit Mt. Everest, as they encountered a very real and tangible obstacle that would prove to be their final hurdle on the way to the top.

When Edmund Hillary and Tenzing Norgay set off to reach the summit of Everest on May 29, 1953, they realized that if they were going to be successful they would need to overcome a number of significant challenges that were in their way. For instance, they knew that the extremely thin air at altitude would make their ascent a slow and difficult one. They also knew that the steep slopes leading to the summit would be physically draining and potentially dangerous. And while the weather was quite good when they left their high camp, they also knew that conditions could change very quickly on the world's highest peak.

For more than three decades, teams of climbers had been looking for a way to conquer Everest. All previous attempts had been turned back due to poor weather, difficult terrain, or the lack of proper equipment. In fact, just three days earlier, two of Hillary and Norgay's teammates—Tom Bourdillon and Charles Evans—were forced to abandon their ascent when they experienced issues with the oxygen masks that allow them to breathe at such high altitudes. At the time they were just 300 feet below the ever-elusive summit, but it might as well have been a mile. Without properly functioning gear, there was no way to get up and down the mountain safely.

After waiting out a storm, Hillary and Norgay launched their own summit bid on May 28, reaching as high as 27,900 feet where they spent a long, cold night in a small tent waiting impatiently for the arrival of daybreak. The following morning, they climbed even higher, eventually passing the point at which Bourdillon and Evans turned back. From then on, they would be hiking in completely unexplored territory, where it was possible they could encounter any number of unknown obstacles that would prevent them from reaching their goal.

The two men made rapid progress and soon found themselves within striking distance of the summit. But before they could take those few remaining steps to the top of the world, there was one final obstacle to overcome. This last hurdle presented itself in the form of a forty-foot tall, sheer rock face with few handholds to grab. It was by far the most technical climbing they had experienced on the entire route. To make matters worse, the imposing wall was flanked by precipitous drops on either side. To the right was a 10,000-foot plummet, while the left was only slightly less intimidating with its 8,000-foot drop. One wrong move could prove disastrous.

If this particular rock face were located at a lower altitude it would prove to be a fairly minor challenge at most. But standing at nearly 29,000 feet, while wearing thirty-pound backpacks, not to mention oxygen tanks and masks, it suddenly became a far more difficult hurdle to get past. Add in the fact that Hillary and Norgay were both cold and exhausted, and suddenly this relatively short forty-foot wall grew into something much larger and even more intimidating. Still, the two men hadn't come all that way just to turn back now.

While examining this final obstacle, Hillary noticed a crack that was visible between the rock itself and the thick coating of snow and ice that covered it. Seeing no other option, he jammed his body into that crack and began to shimmy his way upwards. His considerable experience and talent at rock climbing was put to good use as he slowly, but surely, made his way to the top of the crack, eventually popping out at the top of the wall itself. His companion, who had far less rock climbing experience, followed as best he could, eventually scrambling up the wall as well.

Once the rock face was overcome, the men saw only a narrow ridge leading slightly upwards towards the horizon. The two climbers moved forward and within a matter of minutes they crossed the final few meters to reach the summit itself. They had managed to overcome the last barrier to success and now stood at the highest point on the surface of the Earth, a feat that would put them in the history books and turn them into mountaineering legends.

In the years that followed, the forty-foot rock wall that proved to be the final obstacle on the way to the summit of Everest became known as the Hillary Step, earning it an esteemed place in mountaineering lore. Since Hillary and Norgay made their historic ascent, literally thousands of others have followed in their footsteps, tracing the very same route to the top of the mountain. Upon reaching the Hillary Step, each and every one of those climbers knew that the summit wasn't far off and success was within their grasp. Fortunately for them, they get to climb that famous rock face using fixed ropes and modern gear, rather than ascending it completely by hand.

Sadly, the Hillary Step suffered damage during the devastating earthquake that hit Nepal back in 2015. The once-challenging rock face has now crumbled, altering the path to the summit of Everest forever. The new route is less technical and more accessible, making the mountain a bit safer and easier to climb. Still, the most famous obstacle in high altitude mountaineering will always hold a hallowed place in the history of climbing, a physical representation of having to overcome unexpected challenges in order to rise to the top.

When an obstacle presents itself, it is important to not only acknowledge that it exists, but to also properly categorize it, too. Some of the challenges you'll face will be ones that you can control and plan for, while others will be completely out of your hands, leaving you with few options other than to try to weather the storm and move forward as best you can.

These types of obstacles can be the most frustrating of all, as often times it will feel like your goals are slipping away, even though you haven't necessarily done anything wrong. Setbacks like these can include a wide variety of things, such as scheduling delays, teammates suddenly bowing out of a project, or unexpected injuries when training for an athletic event. They can also involve larger-than-life problems like a significant downturn in the economy, a shifting political climate, or even a natural disaster. Those are all external forces that we can't influence directly, but they could in turn have a significant and lasting impact on our goals.

66

Others can stop you temporarily, you are the only one who can do it permanently."

—John Wooden

Unsurprisingly, the obstacles that are easiest to overcome are those that are within our own direct control. These include things like making more time in our schedules to focus on our goals, or learning new skills that can help us to accomplish the objectives we've set for ourselves. Having the proper motivation and dedication can carry us a long way, allowing us to achieve some very big things simply through persistence and focus alone.

Back in the late 1950s, Bill Bowerman—the legendary track coach at the University of Oregon—found himself unhappy with the current state of running shoes. The athletic footwear of the day was typically made out of thick leather and often featured metal spikes designed to give runners a better grip while competing in their events. Unfortunately, those shoes were also heavy and uncomfortable, often hindering performance as much as they helped.

In an effort to change the way running shoes were made, Bowerman sent letters to several shoe manufacturers, offering tips on ways that they could improve their products. More often than not, those suggestions fell on deaf ears, with none of the major brands even considering the track coach's recommendations.

Frustrated by the stagnation of the footwear industry, Bowerman started to tinker with his own shoe designs instead. At first, he enlisted the help of a local cobbler who provided the skills, training, and knowledge that the coach needed in order to understand how shoes were made. Later, he would also consult with a bootmaker, honing his skills further as he learned to develop his own shoe patterns while unravelling the technical mysteries that came with creating athletic footwear from the ground up. He would even buy the latest running shoes, take them home to his workshop, and immediately run them through his band saw. By cutting them in half, he could see exactly how they were made, which brought further insights into what worked and what didn't.

At first, Bowerman's prototypes were very basic and simple, but as his skills and understanding of shoe manufacturing evolved, his designs started to become more complex too. He experimented with different materials for the sole, tested new fabrics for the upper, and even swapped out metal spikes for ones made of plastic in an effort to discover what combination of design, materials, and craftsmanship worked best.

In the fall of 1958, Bowerman had learned enough about shoemaking that he was ready to start testing his designs on his Oregon track athletes. The first to get a pair of the custom-built footwear was an incoming freshman runner by the name of Phil Knight. Bowerman made a set of running shoes specifically with Knight in mind, custom molding them for his feet. One day, Knight tested them out for the very first time at practice and the unique shoes were soon spotted by his teammates who gathered round to get a closer look. It wasn't long before the new footwear were commandeered by Otis Davis, a talented runner who would eventually win a gold medal in the 400 meters at the 1960 Olympic Games in Rome. He was wearing a pair of Bowerman's shoes when he crossed the finish line in that race.

Despite the fact that he was making serious improvements in terms of weight and performance with his running shoe designs, Bowerman remained frustrated with the athletic footwear industry. His innovative approach to creating shoes—which included using a waffle iron to experiment with a new style of soles—had provided significant gains in terms of comfort and speed. Yet there was still little interest from within the industry to adopt his paradigm-shifting philosophies.

Undeterred, Bowerman and Knight continued to work with one another, improving the coach's shoe designs and testing new models. The two even went into business together, launching a company called Blue Ribbon Sports. Their plan was to import lightweight running shoes from Japan with the hopes that Bowerman might eventually be able to use his own research and development to impact how the Japanese shoes were manufactured.

Eventually Blue Ribbon's relationship with its Japanese partners began to pay dividends. Bowerman continually made suggestions on how the running shoes could be improved, and it wasn't long before the designers in Japan started to listen. One of those recommendations was the inclusion of a two-piece sole that was soft and supportive where it needed to be, and hard and responsive elsewhere, efficiently mixing comfort and performance for the very first time.

When this design was incorporated into a shoe called the Tiger Cortez, it immediately became a hit. The running shoe arrived in the US—via Blue Ribbon Sports—just as the jogging craze was starting to take off, and it became a bestseller almost overnight. A legion of new runners finally had the footwear they needed for long distance events, whether they were racing competitively or were just weekend warriors looking to stay fit.

Realizing they had struck gold with this latest design, Bowerman and Knight decided to dissolve Blue Ribbon and cut ties with their Japanese partners. They were finished with importing shoes that used the technology and innovations that they had helped create. Instead they decided to launch their own athletic footwear company and make their own shoes in the US. They would name this new company Nike. Over the past five decades, it has gone on to become one of the biggest and most dominant brands in all of sports.

Of course, Bowerman didn't know all of this

would come to pass when he first started experimenting with making his own athletic footwear. At the time, all he wanted to do was create shoes that would help his athletes perform at a higher level. In order to do that, he had to learn everything there was to know about making shoes, gaining skills and knowledge that didn't make him a better running coach, but would prove invaluable in achieving his goal of helping his team run faster over both short and long distances.

Throughout his coaching career, Bowerman led the University of Oregon to four NCAA track championships, establishing it as the premiere running program in all of collegiate sports. He also coached some of the best runners that the country has ever produced, including sixteen athletes who could run a sub-four minute mile. Along the way, he managed to completely change the athletic footwear industry, and build Nike into a company that is worth more than $100 billion today.

That is the kind of success that you could reach when you set goals for yourself, identify the obstacles that are in your way, and actively look for options to overcome them. Bowerman knew which variables he couldn't control himself and tenaciously went about finding ways around them. Eventually his patience and persistence paid off, and the rest is history.

Perhaps the biggest obstacle that Bowerman faced when he first began designing shoes was his almost complete lack of knowledge of the athletic apparel business. He overcame that by systematically learning everything he could about how shoes were made, eventually turning himself into an expert in the field. By the time he and Knight launched Nike, he was probably amongst the most knowledgeable people in the world when it came to running shoes.

The moral of the story is that if you want to achieve your goals in life, and overcome big obstacles along the way, knowledge is often the key. Understanding the challenges you'll face will prove invaluable, helping you to not only chart the proper course, but to also spot the biggest obstacles you'll face and discover ways around them.

66

A hero is an ordinary
individual who finds the
strength to persevere
and endure in spite of
overwhelming obstacles."

—Christopher Reeve

On the other hand, studying a problem for too long can also lead to indecision and paralysis. Sometimes the best way to overcome an obstacle is to tackle the challenge head on without overthinking it. This can often turn out to be the fastest and most efficient route, even if it may seem like an extremely daunting approach at first.

For instance, if you want to run a marathon, you can read all kinds of articles and books on what that experience is like. You can memorize training schedules, read countless reviews of running shoes, study dietary plans, and even watch online videos that can help you perfect your running form. In other words, you can turn yourself into an expert on *preparing* to run a marathon, without ever lacing up your shoes and actually going out for a run yourself.

Running a race is both physically and mentally demanding, however, and no amount of studying can change that. If you want to take part in a marathon you'll have to train. There are no shortcuts to the finish line, which means at some point you'll have to stop reading about what it takes to prepare for a long distance competition and actually start the arduous process of learning to run all those miles.

Knowledge and preparation are always key components for overcoming obstacles, but there is something to be said for just putting everything else aside and going after a challenge head on. Sometimes the simplest and most successful approach is to stop looking for ways around the roadblocks in our way and instead look for ways to go through them. This approach isn't always pretty, but it can be very effective.

Boxer James "Buster" Douglas used this tactic and ended up stunning the world, pulling off what some believe to be the greatest upset in sports history. He went on to be an inspiration to millions, and is a good example of what you can achieve when you put your mind to it.

Throughout the 1980s, Douglas was a journeyman heavyweight fighter who was known to be a tough competitor when properly motivated. That said, he also had several inexplicable losses on his resume to boxers who were not as skilled or physically gifted as he was. Still, he managed to work his way up the ranks, and in February of 1990, he earned a title shot against Mike Tyson, who was the undisputed heavyweight champion of the world at the time.

It is almost impossible to overstate just how dominant Tyson was in the prime of his career. A ferocious fighter who mixed tremendous power and unbelievable hand speed, Tyson became the youngest heavyweight champion ever by claiming the World Boxing Council title in 1986 at the age of twenty. A year later, he added the World Boxing Association and International Boxing Federation championship belts to his resume as well, earning the "undisputed champion" moniker. Over the next three years, Tyson went on to decimate pretty much every fighter that was put in front of him, compiling a record of thirty-seven wins and no losses.

In contrast to Tyson's success, Douglas had a rocky road on his way to the title match. He had fought for the heavyweight championship against Tony Tucker in 1987, but lost that bout by technical knockout in the tenth round. He won his next six fights however, which put him amongst the top ten heavyweights in the world, drawing the attention of Tyson's management team. The champ's handlers no doubt saw Douglas as an easy payday and a tune-up fight before taking on number one contender Evander Holyfield.

The fight between Tyson and Douglas was set to take place on February 11, 1990, at the Tokyo Dome in Japan. But three weeks before the bout was scheduled to go down, Douglas's mom suffered a stroke and passed away unexpectedly. For a time, it looked like the matchup was in jeopardy, with the challenger considering backing out. But despite his grief, Douglas decided to uphold his agreement and meet Tyson in the ring.

In the days leading up to the showdown, Las Vegas oddsmakers were so convinced that Tyson would dispatch Douglas with ease that most of them didn't even post odds on the fight. The one exception was The Mirage Casino, which listed the challenger as a 42-to-1 underdog. Boxing experts tended to agree with that assessment, with most going on record as saying it would be an easy win for the champ.

That wasn't exactly how things played out in

the Tokyo Dome, however, as the tone of the fight was very different right from the outset. Boxing fans were accustomed to seeing Tyson rush across the ring and attack his opponent with an unrelenting barrage of punches that left many of them down for the count within the first round. This time out, Tyson advanced on Douglas only to be met with quick, accurate jabs that managed to keep the champion at bay. The shorter Tyson was unable to get through the challenger's defenses and soon became frustrated with his inability to land his usual combinations of power punches.

Perhaps most importantly, Douglas wasn't intimidated in any way by his opponent. Tyson's fearsome reputation for destroying his challengers often had many boxers feeling defeated long before they ever stepped foot in the ring. His ferocious persona intimidated them to such a degree that most entered the match just hoping to still be standing at the end. This tentative approach, coupled with a fear of getting knocked out, meant that Tyson had rarely ever been tested. His opponents simply refused to go at him head-on or stand toe-to-toe with him in the squared circle.

66

The greatest glory in
living lies not in never
falling, but in rising
every time we fall."

—Nelson Mandela

Because he was such an overwhelming underdog, Douglas came into the fight with nothing to lose. None of the so-called boxing experts gave him much of a chance, so the worst that could happen would be that he got knocked out, and they would all say that things went exactly as expected. But if he could give the champ a good fight, it might just change their perspective to some degree.

Being a 42-to-1 underdog was surprisingly liberating for the challenger, who was still grieving over the loss of his mother. That helped to put the fight into perspective to some degree as well, reminding Douglas that this wasn't life or death. He could win or lose, but at the end of the day he would go back home to his family and friends and continue on as he always had. That wasn't the case for his mom, who had always been in his corner.

Most of the men who faced Tyson did so by moving backwards while he relentlessly hunted them down, cutting off the ring until they had nowhere to go. It was then that he would unleash one of his trademark attacks, which tended to leave most opponents on the ground in a heap. Douglas didn't move backwards however but instead did what no other fighter before him had tried with Tyson—he moved forward.

For Douglas, Tyson had become the obstacle that he knew that he had to take on directly. Other fighters had tried to use finesse and speed to stay away from the champion, but ultimately that proved fruitless. The challenger's tactic this time wasn't to back up or try to stay away, but instead to take the fight to Tyson, who had once proclaimed that he was the "baddest man on the planet."

Prior to the Douglas fight, Tyson was seen somewhat as a bully in the ring who was able to impose his will through intimidation and fear. That wasn't the case in Tokyo, however, and it soon became apparent that his challenger wasn't afraid of losing or getting embarrassed in the ring. Instead, he was focused, fought within his own limits, and wouldn't allow Tyson to push him around. It wasn't long before the hunter became the hunted, and it was Douglas who was dominating the match and forcing the champion to reevaluate his tactics.

In the end, Douglas would go on to defeat the man who had been all but invincible up until that point. After surviving a controversial knockdown in the eighth round, the challenger was able to get back on his feet, collect himself, and take the fight back to Tyson. In the tenth round the tables turned, as Douglas was able to knock the champion down with a bone-jarring uppercut followed by a combination of four more punches. It was the first time in Tyson's career that he had ever hit the canvas and he would not get back up.

In a matter of moments James "Buster" Douglas went from being just another good fighter who had never completely lived up to his potential, to becoming the heavyweight champion of the world. Those who watched the fight as it unfolded were completely stunned, as the massive underdog was able to defy all of the odds and win a match that seemed un-winnable. And he did so not by trying to find a way around his obstacle but by going straight at him instead.

Make no mistake, Douglas trained hard for the fight. He studied film, sparred with tough fighters, ran countless miles, and learned everything he could about the man he would face in Tokyo. But every fighter that Tyson faced up until that point had done the same thing and they all failed in the process.

Most of us will never have to take on an opponent as formidable as Mike Tyson in the prime of his career. Our obstacles are likely to be far more intangible, although they may not be any less intimidating. Still, there is something to be learned from the approach Douglas took for that fight. He didn't look for ways to avoid his foe, or to divert from the plan that he and his trainers had created. Instead, he methodically moved forward, straight at the man who had dispatched every other boxer that he had faced. In the end, that proved to be a winning strategy, and Tyson's aura of invincibility was shattered forever.

What we can take away from Buster Douglas's story is that achieving big things isn't always easy, but it is all but impossible if you don't properly identify the obstacles in front of you, formulate a plan of action, and then execute that strategy. Avoiding the challenges we face only delays the inevitable. At some point, you'll have to find a way to get past whatever foe is standing in your way, or you will find yourself doomed to failure.

It is also important to remember that inaction, hesitation, and uncertainty are some of the biggest obstacles that keep us from achieving everything that we want in life. It is far better to have tried and failed than to not have tried at all. Optimally, those failures won't result in us quitting, but will make us stronger and more resilient instead. The knowledge and experience that is gained along the way often allows us to get back on our feet and continue pressing forward towards our goals.

By learning from those experiences, we can also learn to identify the biggest obstacles in our lives and better understand how to overcome them. When we learn to do that, we never truly fail at anything in life and only get stronger as a result.

"

Obstacles are those frightful things you see when you take your eyes off your goal"

—Henry Ford

PART II

GETTING OUT OF YOUR OWN WAY

In order to become a Navy SEAL, prospective candidates must first complete a rigorous program known as Basic Underwater Demolition/SEAL training, or BUD/S for short. This six-month-long course is conducted at the Naval Special Warfare Training Center in Coronado, California, and consists of three individual phases, each designed to take a class of relatively raw recruits and turn them into the toughest and best-trained fighters on the planet.

Phase One is a seven-week-long program that focuses on physical and mental conditioning, culminating with the SEALs legendary Hell Week. During that five and a half day period, candidates are pushed to their absolute limits, experiencing very little sleep, traveling more than 200 miles on foot, and continually training for as long as twenty hours per day. It is a grueling experience that was intentionally created to separate those who have the potential to graduate and become SEALs from those who simply don't have what it takes to join the Navy's elite warriors.

This phase of BUD/S will make nearly every individual question his own strength and resolve, with many asking themselves why they are bothering to continue with the training on an almost daily basis. Those who quit generally do so not because they can't handle the physical challenges, but because they are not mentally tough enough to push through the adversity. Those who do continue almost invariably come out the other side much stronger and more confident than they were when they started.

After surviving Phase One, the SEAL candidates are far better prepared for Phases Two and Three of BUD/S, and as a result the success rate rises dramatically for those who continue on. During Phase Two, SEAL candidates spend eight weeks focused almost exclusively on learning the intricacies of diving and conducting underwater operations. The final phase dedicates nine weeks of training to land warfare, with a particular focus on hand-to-hand combat, small weapons skills, and squad tactics designed to help the men function more as a team. Throughout these phases the physical training continues to ramp up as well, with a high emphasis placed on a SEAL's ability to adapt and overcome any challenges that are placed in his way.

Once they have graduated from BUD/S, the candidates are one step closer to becoming SEALs, but they haven't earned the right to join those elite ranks quite yet. First, they must complete a three week course in basic parachute training, which adds the "air" to a SEAL's sea, air, and land acronym. From there, it is on to the eight-week SEAL Qualification Training (SQT) program, which completes the indoctrination of the candidate and prepares them for assignment to one of the SEAL teams.

By that point in their training, the candidates have already proven that they have the physical and mental toughness necessary to become a SEAL and are instead focused on learning new skills, honing their existing talents, and gaining experience in mission planning, tactical preparation, and advanced military procedures. In other words, the training officers are putting a fine edge on each individual, taking them from a blunt instrument to a highly-trained professional.

After completing all of that training, the candidates finally earn the right to pin the Special Warfare Insignia to their uniforms. This distinctive and much-coveted badge indicates that the wearer has successfully completed BUD/S and has joined the ranks of the Navy SEALs at long last. It is without a doubt one of the proudest moments of their career and a symbol of excellence that sticks with them for the rest of their lives.

Many of the candidates that enter BUD/S do so with a sense of confidence and swagger. Most of the persons accepted into the SEAL training program have already shown themselves to be exceptionally gifted in terms of athletic ability, intelligence, and drive. They understand that they are about to attempt something that is incredibly difficult, but since they haven't ever been completely pushed to their limits, they fully expect to make it through just fine. The vast majority of them are wrong.

On average, only about 20 percent of the individuals who enter a BUD/S class actually make it through Phase One of training. Those that do move on from the rigorous seven-week program do so because they are willing to let go of the preconceptions they had about themselves at the start of their training, and instead begin to see themselves for who they truly are. In most cases, that means learning that they are actually stronger and more resilient than they ever imagined. That can be a liberating feeling to say the least, allowing individuals to achieve great things on their own and to rise to even greater heights while working as a part of a team.

Having the ability to shake off the preconceptions that we have of ourselves is an important part of being able to achieve our objectives in life. Many of us lack a complete understanding of what we are truly capable of, which can lead to roadblocks that prevent us from reaching our goals. Many of those roadblocks come from within ourselves, which is why it is incredibly important to learn how to put them behind us and get out of our own way. Because realistically speaking, we often find ways to sabotage our own success and prevent ourselves from achieving everything we could or should in life.

There are so many ways that we can get in the way of our own progress that it is tough to know even where to begin. In most cases, we end up stumbling over our own two feet—figuratively speaking at least—in part because we have a lack of understanding of exactly what we are, and aren't, capable of. Knowing where your physical and mental boundaries truly lie allows you to not only operate within a clearly defined zone, but it also helps you to learn when you can push yourself further and harder, as well as when you need to back off and reassess your approach to an obstacle.

These are the kind of lessons that SEAL candidates learn during their Phase One training. Through that rigorous program, they start to identify the limits of their mental and physical abilities and then slowly but surely explore those limits more fully. In most cases, they discover that they are capable of amazing things that even they didn't realize were possible. This is what eventually allows them to survive Hell Week and complete their BUD/S training.

"

Everyone has their own
Everest to climb."

—Wanda Rutkiewicz

Most people will not have the opportunity to take part in BUD/S training to help them define exactly where their own limits are found. If we truly want to succeed, however, exploring those boundaries will play a crucial role. In order to avoid obstacles of our own making, we must first develop a clear image of who we are and what we can do. When we do that, we can also learn to more accurately assess our talents, setting ourselves up for a higher degree of success.

In some cases, we tend to overestimate our own abilities, both natural and acquired. This can cause us to crash and burn when we finally attempt something truly difficult or step outside our traditional comfort zones for the first time. Without a realistic understanding of where our talents actually lie, we can come away with an overabundance of self-confidence, although the truth is that confidence is often built on a house of cards. If those cards ever come tumbling down, it can be devastating to our morale and sense of self-worth.

A runner can experience this when they decide to compete in a race for the very first time. Many athletes use a GPS fitness watch to help them train, recording their speed, distance, and time so that they can analyze how much progress they are making. That data can be a very helpful tool for understanding your strengths and weaknesses, although it can also instill a false sense of confidence, too.

Fast workout times can be misleading, in part because the runner is only competing against the elapsed time on his or her watch and not another human being. Knowing how fast you run is helpful when preparing for a race of course, but it isn't always a good indication of just how well you'll do on the day of the event. Running a sub-seven-minute mile while working out may feel quick and effortless, giving you the sense that you'll be the fastest runner out on the course. But when you meet the runner who can easily run a sub-six-minute mile, it can crush your confidence and leave you questioning your abilities.

More often than not, however, it isn't a feeling of over confidence that causes us to stumble on our way to our goals. In fact, it is usually a complete lack of confidence that prevents us from more aggressively pursuing the objectives we've set for ourselves. There are few things more paralyzing in life than not believing in yourself, which usually ends up keeping us squarely inside our comfort zones, never straying far from the safety of our sheltered lives. After all, if we're not smart enough, talented enough, or dedicated enough to go after the things we want, why should we even try?

As it turns out, many of us are indeed smart and talented enough to reach the goals that we've set for ourselves; we just don't always believe that is the case. As a result, we create our own hurdles, which end up serving as excuses as to why we shouldn't pursue the things we truly want out of life. In other words, we are our own worst enemies at times, sabotaging our own path to success.

Learning to get out of your own way and clear a path to your goals is never easy, but it is essential. One of the first keys to doing that is being able to accurately assess your own skills, talents, and abilities. Overestimating your strengths can lead to failure just as quickly as underestimating what you are truly capable of. That is why it is vitally important to not only get to know your own boundaries, but also be brutally honest about what you can and can't do. Armed with that knowledge, you'll not only be able to better take on the challenges you'll face, but will also know when you can forge on alone and when it is best to partner up with others in order to achieve your goals.

Apple Inc. co-founder Steve Wozniak was a talented, yet shy and introverted, engineer who, in the 1970s, designed some of the most innovative and groundbreaking circuit boards for early personal computers. Woz, as he was known to his friends, was ahead of his time when it came to building microcomputer systems, developing and creating the internal hardware and software completely on his own. He loved to tinker with electronics of all kinds, but never really saw much of a potential market to sell his devices.

Wozniak's legendary partner was Steve Jobs. While not as technically gifted as Woz, he was far more of a visionary. He also happened to be more gregarious and outgoing, which came in handy when it came time to start selling the Apple I computer, Wozniak's first breakthrough device.

Before forming Apple, Wozniak was an engineer for tech giant Hewlett Packard, where he worked on advanced scientific calculators. According to Woz himself, he offered HP the designs for his personal computer no less than five times, but on each occasion his supervisors declined his offers. As a result, Wozniak was free to do what he wanted with his highly technical circuit board plans.

By all accounts it was Jobs who was the first to see the real potential of the Apple I, immediately recognizing that he and Woz could sell the systems to technology enthusiasts across the country. Up until that time there were no affordable off-the-shelf personal computers on the market, so most programmers were forced to build their own. The Apple I would be a breakout product with the computer science and engineering crowd, many of whom had been waiting for years for just such a device to come along.

In the early days of Apple, Jobs and Wozniak would often attend technology conventions and visit home brew computer clubs to demo their device. Invariably, it would be Woz who assembled the system and sat at the keyboard, while Jobs would handle the speaking duties, fielding questions, extolling the virtues of owning a home computer, and evangelizing the technology revolution that was to come.

In a lot of ways, Jobs and Wozniak were polar opposites of one another and yet they still managed to complement each other extremely well. Without Jobs's ability to get others excited about using technology, Wozniak's personal computer may never have gotten off the ground. He likely would have remained a talented engineer toiling away in obscurity at Hewlett Packard. On the other hand, without Woz's groundbreaking tech, Jobs may not have come up with the idea of creating a computer company that would go on to literally change the world.

66

The only person you are
destined to become is the
person you decide to be."

—Ralph Waldo Emerson

The two men did share one trait in common; they both had a good understanding of their individual strengths and weaknesses, and why they needed each other to succeed. The introverted Wozniak wasn't good at selling his ideas to others, while Jobs could sell ice to eskimos if given the chance. But as visionary as he was, Jobs wasn't an engineer and couldn't actually create the technology he was selling without Wozniak's help. In the end, they both recognized the fact that their relationship was mutually beneficial, making it one of the most iconic business partnerships of all time.

Another important step in learning how to get out of your own way is confronting the doubts you have about your own abilities. That is easier to do when you have an accurate assessment of your strengths and weaknesses, as you'll have a better understanding of just how well-suited you are to take on the challenges that you'll face along the way. In theory, knowing exactly what you're good at should help to build a higher, more stable sense of confidence that will allow you to pursue your goals. In reality, however, we all know that isn't necessarily the case.

Generally speaking, the uncertainty that we experience when thinking about the objectives we've defined for ourselves almost always stem directly from fear. Usually it is a fear of failure that holds us back, as we think about the consequences that come from not being able to accomplish the things we set out to do. The whispers of negativity that reverberate through our brains are some of the most powerful and counterproductive thoughts that we can have, often paralyzing us into inaction. Learning how to ignore those thoughts and move on is crucial if we ever want to find a measure of success.

Make no mistake, every SEAL candidate experiences those same feelings of self-doubt at some point during their BUD/S training. By its very nature the program is designed to shake their confidence and make them question their ability to continue on to Phase Two. Those who can't find a way to silence the whispers of doubt are the ones who are most likely to end up ringing the bell signifying their desire to quit. On the other hand, the candidates who are mentally strong, know that they have the skills to continue on, and are committed to seeing the program through to the end, already have the mindset needed to become a Navy SEAL.

It has been said that 90 percent of SEAL training is mental and the other 10 percent is physical. The same could be said about overcoming just about any obstacle in our life, as more often than not the barriers that we create for ourselves mostly come from the dark recesses of our own minds. When we learn to ignore the whispers, embrace our own strengths and talents, and keep our eyes firmly focused on the goals we have created, great things can happen. After that, the doubt begins to melt away and an influx of confidence will come in to take its place.

"

The only victory that counts is the one over yourself."

—Jesse Owens

There are few people on the planet who are as successful as Warren Buffett. The businessman and investor has made billions of dollars over the course of his career by shrewdly divining where and when to focus his attention and considerable assets. His insights and wisdom are so valued by Wall Street insiders that an endorsement from Buffett can make or break the fortunes of established companies and startups alike.

Buffet has been the Chairman and CEO—not to mention largest shareholder—of Berkshire Hathaway since its founding in 1970. The holding company is a multinational conglomerate that is valued at more than $700 billion, owning such brands as Dairy Queen, Helzberg Diamonds, and Geico Insurance outright. Through the firm, Buffett has also invested heavily in companies like Coca-Cola, American Express, and Apple.

With such a successful track record, you would think that Buffett was a man of great confidence and resolve from the very beginning. That wasn't the case, however, and when he started his career as a stockbroker, he suffered from a paralyzing fear of public speaking. In fact, Buffett himself has said that as a college student, he dreaded even standing up in front of the class and uttering his own name. This fear was so ingrained in him that while attending the famous Wharton School of Business at the University of Pennsylvania, he went to great lengths to avoid taking classes that would require him to give a speech or answer questions aloud.

After he graduated from college and embarked upon his business career, Buffett recognized that his fear of speaking in public was holding him back. He accurately assessed his own strengths and weaknesses, and while even at a relatively young age he demonstrated an uncanny knack for knowing where to invest money, he also knew that if he couldn't get over his phobia for speaking in front of a crowd, that he probably wouldn't achieve all of the success that he expected of himself.

For a time, Buffett simply avoided any situation that would require him to stand in front of a large group and talk to them about investing their money. That worked for awhile, but as word of his success continued to spread, the requests for him to speak only grew in number. Eventually he realized that he needed to confront his fears head on if he was ever going to get past them. So, he enrolled in a Dale Carnegie course on public speaking where he was relieved to find that he wasn't the only one who hated the idea of standing in front of others to give a presentation.

Eventually Buffett graduated from that course and mustered up enough confidence to start speaking in public. In fact, not long after that, he began teaching a class on the basic principles of investment at the University of Nebraska-Omaha. His course would soon become a very popular one and many of the students who signed up for it turned out to be more than twice his age.

Today Buffett is estimated to be worth more than $80 billion, which makes him one of the richest men on the planet. Unsurprisingly he gets requests to speak in public all of the time, often sharing his insights with other investors, or imparting wisdom to young college students. Those speaking engagements are, of course, much easier now, but they only became more tolerable thanks to Buffet's acknowledgment of his fear and weakness, and more importantly, his willingness to do something about it. Rather than avoiding the thing that he most feared he instead embraced it, moved outside his comfort zone, and learned to deal with his phobia head on. Those are the kinds of traits that help us to not only get out of our own way, but also find success in the process.

"

He who is not courageous
enough to take risks
will accomplish
nothing in life."

—Muhammad Ali

While fear and uncertainty are extremely counter-productive to our success, if there is a trait that is a close second in creating barriers to our achievements, it is probably our ability to procrastinate. As human beings we naturally want to avoid doing the tasks that are difficult and demanding, in favor of activities that are easier and much more enjoyable. We will even go to great lengths to fabricate a series of other things to do in order to avoid dealing with the ones that we know will be harder to complete. In other words, we are once again finding ways to get in our own way by creating obstacles that prevent us from reaching our goals.

Procrastination is often another symptom that stems from a fear of failure. We're so afraid that the decisions we make won't be the right ones that we avoid them altogether. Often the feeling is that if we don't deal with those challenges head on, perhaps they'll resolve themselves on their own over time and we won't have to deal with them at all.

Occasionally this proves to be an effective

strategy that only ends up reinforcing our bad habit of procrastinating. More often than not, however, it only delays the inevitable. Eventually we have to deal with the tough choices and difficult tasks, but since we've avoided them for longer than we should have, we often end up facing them with a looming deadline. That only serves to cause more stress and anxiety, as we then struggle to achieve our objectives in a shorter span of time and with fewer resources, which usually isn't a recipe for success.

When a competitive athlete begins training for an event, the rigorous training schedule can be difficult to maintain and requires a high level of commitment and sacrifice. It means giving up free time with friends and family to focus instead on getting physically and mentally prepared for the competition. Often times it also requires adhering to a strict diet and sleep schedule in an effort to get as fit and prepared as possible too. In other words, it is a difficult, demanding process that may result in success, but isn't exactly an enjoyable one to embark upon.

Naturally, most people will put off starting such a program for as long as possible. They want to enjoy the creature comforts of life while not choosing to push their bodies any harder than they have to. We'll tell ourselves that we can start the program next week and still have plenty of time later. The reality is that it would be much better to start early and give your body the time it needs to adjust to the demands that are being placed on it.

By procrastinating, the athlete may not give themselves the necessary time required to get fully prepared for the competition, which generally results in diminished performance. In order to be successful, they shouldn't avoid the training schedule, but must instead embrace it. Otherwise they'll find it much harder to achieve their goals and will ultimately only be letting themselves down.

It is important to point out that procrastination doesn't equate to laziness. Plenty of highly successful, hard-working people still find themselves avoiding certain tasks from time to time simply because they don't want to have to deal with them at that moment. It is not uncommon for even very talented and intelligent individuals to backburner their work simply because they don't have the motivation or drive to focus in on a particular project in a timely fashion.

"

My advice is to never do tomorrow what you can do today. Procrastination is the thief of time."

—Charles Dickens

Frank Lloyd Wright is arguably the most famous and influential architect of all time, but he was also known to be a procrastinator. He would often put off working on a new design for weeks and even months at a time, preferring to focus on other things instead. One of the more famous stories that illustrates this involves one of Wright's most celebrated projects, a house called Fallingwater, which is located in Mill Run, Pennsylvania.

As the story goes, the architect was commissioned to design a country home for Edgar Kaufmann, a Pittsburgh businessman who made his fortune by operating a chain of department stores. Kaufmann owned a secluded piece of land that was thickly wooded and featured a magnificent waterfall. He asked Wright to create a building that integrated seamlessly with the rural setting, while also being modern, innovative, and visually striking at the same time.

Wright visited the site where the house would be built, made some notes, and inspected the grounds.

After surveying the premises, the architect promised Kaufmann he would get to work on the project as soon as possible. After that, Wright returned to his office in Wisconsin, presumably ready to get down to work.

But over the ensuing weeks and months Kaufmann heard very little from Wright. When the tycoon inquired about the progress of the design of his new house, the architect simply told him that the work was progressing as planned and he would have something to share soon. Over time, however, Kaufmann became impatient and decided to pay Wright a visit to check up on his work firsthand, giving the designer just a few hours' notice of his impending arrival.

As it turns out, Wright hadn't even put pen to paper yet and had no designs ready to show his client. He had simply come home from visiting the Pennsylvania countryside and never went to work on the promised schematics. With no hard deadline for delivering the final plans, and Kaufmann affording him plenty of freedom, the famous architect had never gotten around to actually working on the new house at all.

When Wright learned that Kaufmann was on the way to his office, the deadline moved from some nebulous point in the future to just a few hours away. Reportedly, the architect sat down and enjoyed a leisurely breakfast before moving into his studio and starting work. As legend has it, he spent two hours sketching up his ideas for a house that would naturally integrate with the stunningly beautiful Pennsylvania property, creating drawings of his ideas as they came to him.

When Kaufman arrived he was suitably impressed with what Wright had to show him. His doubts were put to rest and he told the architect to continue with his work. The house that he designed would eventually go on to be called Fallingwater, after the waterfall that is found on the property. Today, the building is widely considered to be one of the greatest pieces of architecture that Frank Lloyd Wright—or anyone else for that matter—has ever created.

Most of us don't have the experience, technical abilities, and natural talent of a Frank Lloyd Wright to bail us out if we procrastinate for too long. While his impromptu meeting with Kaufmann turned into one of the most famous buildings ever designed, that same situation is much more likely to end in disaster for the rest of us. A supremely gifted individual may be able to snatch victory from the jaws of defeat every now and then, but eventually the odds will catch up with us and we'll find ourselves not just out of luck, but also out of time.

Wright isn't the only famous person who is or was plagued with procrastination issues. Wolfgang Amadeus Mozart reportedly put off composing the overture for *Don Giovanni* until the night before the opening of the opera, preventing the orchestra from even rehearsing it ahead of time. Writer Victor Hugo was notoriously so bad at meeting deadlines that he ordered his servants to hide his clothing so that he wouldn't be tempted to go out at night. Even the Dalai Lama is said to have been a major procrastinator in his days as a student, often arriving late to meetings and routinely turning in his work after the deadline had passed.

The work habits of these individuals didn't just have an impact on their own lives, however, but those around them too. How do you think the members of Mozart's orchestra felt about receiving their sheet music just hours before the curtain lifted? Meanwhile, Hugo's editor and publisher were likely exasperated by his inability to meet deadlines or make meaningful progress on his next book. When we procrastinate, we're often impacting the work and quality of life of those around us, limiting their abilities to achieve their objectives too.

You can add Leonardo Da Vinci to the list of famous procrastinators as well. The famed artist is responsible for some of the greatest works of art the world has ever seen, but he also struggled with completing his projects in a timely fashion. If you commissioned a work of art from the Italian Renaissance man, you needed to have plenty of patience. The *Mona Lisa* is Da Vinci's most famous painting, but it took him sixteen years to complete it. He spent another four years painting the ceiling in the Sistine Chapel and thirteen years on the *Virgin of the Rocks*.

If you need further proof of Da Vinci's propensity to procrastinate, look no further than the countless sketchbooks, scrap papers, notes, and scrolls that he left behind. When he died in 1519, his workshop was filled with drawings, paintings, and other works of art that were in varying stages of completion. This of course begs the question, how many other great works could he have completed were he able to stay on task and finish a project?

In the case of Da Vinci, and many other people who procrastinate, the challenge isn't about having the talent and abilities to get a job done, but rather the focus to see it through to the end. Being able to stay focused and on track is one of the keys for getting out of your own way and giving yourself the best chance for success. Staying focused means being able to drown out distractions, prioritize tasks, and eliminate excuses. It also means being disciplined enough to get down to work in a timely fashion.

There are a number of techniques and tools that you can use to help avoid procrastination, but the reality is that it usually comes down to having discipline and drive. You can set calendar reminders and give yourself artificial deadlines, but those techniques tend to only work for a short time. You can even tell yourself that you work best while under pressure, convincing yourself that waiting until the last minute helps with creativity and productivity. The truth is, those types of strategies are rarely effective for the long term and usually lose value the more often you use them.

In the end, we must learn to confront the tasks head on and remain focused on the most efficient way to handle the challenges we face. When we stop putting things off, and focus on getting down to work, we'll gain a better understand of just how much time is actually wasted due to procrastination. Chances are, you'll be amazed at what you can actually accomplish simply by channeling your time and energy more directly.

Eliminating the old habits—such as the proclivity to procrastinate—is never easy. It not only requires a desire to make a change, but the discipline to see the process of change through to the end. The ability to identify the self-defeating habits that we have in our life and then deciding to replace them with more positive ones is a common trait amongst successful people and plays a key role in overcoming obstacles and achieving goals.

Once again, this requires a good understanding of your own personal strengths and weaknesses as you can't change a bad habit that you can't even identify within yourself. Self-reflection plays an important role in learning to get out of our own way, as it helps us to see the things about ourselves that are holding us back, while also helping us to identify a road map to make the changes we want.

"

When you take risks you learn that there will be times when you succeed and times when you fail, and both are equally important."

—Ellen DeGeneres

Canadian ultrarunner Ray Zahab is the perfect example of this. In his younger days, Zahab enjoyed carousing at all hours of the night, staying out late drinking with friends, and eating foods that were unhealthy. He also smoked a pack of cigarettes a day and generally led a sedentary lifestyle. Those poor habits had him on the road to disaster, which could have ended very badly.

In 1998, Ray made the decision to quit smoking and start taking better care of himself, realizing that if he wanted to live a long and happy life, he probably needed to make some important changes. Two years later, on New Year's Day 2000, he went for a hike with his brother and came home feeling completely enthused about the experience. The sense of adventure and connection with nature was incredibly inspiring, eventually leading him to take up running. He didn't know it at the time, but that tiny decision ended up having an incredibly dramatic impact on the direction of his life, taking him to places he never thought possible.

Like most novice runners, Zahab started slowly and covered relatively short distances. But as the weeks and months passed, he could feel the positive effects this change in lifestyle was starting to have on his body. He also quickly learned that he had a knack for running long distances and it wasn't long before he was competing in marathons and ultra-marathons. He even took part in some of the most challenging and iconic races on the planet, including the Badwater Ultra—which takes place in Death Valley in the middle of July—and the Marathon des Sables, a grueling six-day race across the Sahara Desert in Morocco.

As challenging as those events were, however, they were nothing compared to what was to come. In 2006, Ray, along with ultra runners Charlie Engle and Kevin Lin, embarked on an epic undertaking as they set out to cover the length of the Sahara Desert on foot. The journey would eventually take 111 days for them to complete, covering 4,300 miles across Northern Africa. Zahab and his companions began their quest at the Atlantic Ocean in Senegal and ended on the shores of the Red Sea in Egypt, passing through Mali, Niger, and Libya along the way.

Crossing a desert the size and scope of the Sahara on foot is no easy undertaking, but to do so in just 111 days is especially difficult. That means that the three ultrarunners had to average nearly thirty-nine miles per day, each and every day, through one of the driest and hottest environments on the planet. That is an impressive accomplishment for any athlete, but especially someone who once smoked like a chimney and cared little about his health.

One of the best ways to break yourself of bad habits is to replace those habits with new ones that help you to be more productive. That's exactly what Ray Zahab did when he quit smoking and decided to take up running instead. At the time, his goal was simply to lead a healthier lifestyle and to get into better shape, but that decision altered his life in such dramatic ways that he is now seen as one of the premiere adventure athletes on the planet. In fact, his ability to travel for long distances in remote locations has allowed him to run for a cumulative total of more than 8,700 miles across the Earth's deserts alone. He has even traveled on foot to the South Pole, crossing Antarctica without the use of skis.

As we've examined the various ways that we can learn to get out of our own way and achieve the success we seek in life, one personality trait seems to stand out above all others. Self-discipline plays a crucial role in accomplishing our objectives, helping us to stay focused, on task, and moving forward even in the face of adversity. That alone is usually enough to give you a leg up on the competition, setting yourself up for success in business, athletics, and just about every other aspect of your life.

Discipline plays an important part in the life of a Navy SEAL, too. From the first day of BUD/S to the time they leave the service, a SEAL must train hard, continue to learn new things, and take on some of the most daunting challenges of any military unit on the planet. In order to do that, a SEAL must maintain a high level of discipline at all times, striving to get better in every aspect of the job. The hours are long, the days off are few and far between, and public recognition is almost completely nonexistent, but discipline is still the fuel that fires a SEAL's engines, pushing them forward even when they are exhausted, injured, or close to the edge.

For a SEAL, discipline isn't just part of the job, it

is a way of life. Being focused and in control serves them well both in training and while conducting an operation. Working in conjunction with his team, a SEAL can accomplish great things, even in the face of overwhelming odds, thanks to the discipline that is obtained through hard work, continuous preparation, and sheer force of will.

You don't have to go through BUD/S training in order to develop the self-discipline you need to be successful in life. In fact, the process can be distilled to a few basic principles, which can in turn be learned and honed over time. With a bit of patience, determination, and focus, you can use that same process to build a tough mindset that will allow you to stop getting in your own way and get on track to reaching your objectives.

The first step in that process is setting goals for yourself. Most of us already do this on some level, but it is important to make those goals more of a priority rather than some nebulous thing we would like to accomplish at an indeterminate point in the future. Instead, put those objectives front and center, and start making plans for how they can be achieved. Not making a goal a priority is just another way that we sabotage our own success.

Next, visualize how you can make that goal a reality. In your mind, start to run through the various scenarios that can lead you to success, examining the obstacles that might crop up along the way. Think about the ways that you can deal with those challenges as they arise, analyzing the different ways to approach and overcome any road block. By seeing yourself actually achieving your goals, you'll start to make them more of a reality.

Remaining positive in the face of adversity can be a challenge, particularly when it seems like the world is conspiring to prevent us from reaching our goals. Don't be afraid to give yourself a pep talk on a regular basis, focusing on your strengths and the positive traits that you bring to the table. Avoid dwelling on the negative, and instead stay focused on the course you've charted to your goals. This can be a surprisingly useful technique that can help you to stay upbeat and on task when things start to get difficult.

Finally, learn to not panic when things don't go

your way. Take deep breaths, keep a positive mind-set, and start thinking about how you can get back on track and moving in the right direction. Adversity is a part of the process and strength comes from overcoming the obstacles that get in our path.

"

If you are going to
achieve excellence in big
things, you develop the
habit in little matters.
Excellence is not an
exception, it is a
prevailing attitude."

—Colin Powell

Once the goal has been established, start thinking about all of the steps you'll need to complete in order to reach the larger objective. These bite-sized micro-goals are much easier to comprehend and manage, helping to prevent us from becoming overwhelmed with the enormity of the task at hand. They also serve as the road map that we can follow on our way to achieving that goal, providing some much-needed organization and direction. When one micro-goal is reached, move on to the next, slowly but surely progressing towards the finish line.

When a SEAL candidate embarks on Hell Week, thinking about surviving to the end of the grueling training session can be extremely overwhelming. After all, they'll be tasked with running, swimming, climbing, and paddling almost nonstop for five and a half days, most of which is spent wet, cold, and exhausted. It is enough to cause anyone to reconsider whether or not they have the will to finish BUD/S and proceed on to the next stage of the SEAL training program.

Those who are successful during Hell Week don't allow themselves the luxury of thinking about getting to the end. Instead, they'll break down the process into micro-goals, focusing on just completing the current training exercise, whether it be a long run, swim, series of sit-ups or push-ups, and so on. Only after they have completed that task will they start to consider the next one, without ever looking too far down the road. By breaking down each stage of the exercise into these micro goals it is much easier to stay focused and avoid getting overwhelmed.

By that point of their training, the SEAL candidates have begun to understand the things they need to do in order to be successful. They've figured out how to get out of their own way as they eliminate bad habits, build self-discipline, and gain confidence in their own abilities. Those are the tools that will take them from raw trainees to finely-tuned warriors who are as physically and mentally tough as they come.

Those same tools can help us to accomplish the things we want to achieve in life, too. You may not be conducting covert missions in remote corners of the globe like a Navy SEAL, but you can still use their same techniques to reach your goals. Stay disciplined, stay positive, and stay focused, and you'll find it increasingly easier to get out of your own way. When you can do that, you'll also discover that you can achieve just about anything you set your mind to.

PART III

FINDING SUCCESS

If you were to survey a hundred successful people and ask them what qualities they possess that help them the most when it comes to accomplishing their goals, chances are you would get a hundred different answers. Simply put, there isn't a clear-cut roadmap that you can follow on your way to achieving your objectives. That said, there are a few qualities that seem to be common denominators amongst highly-accomplished people, which can help us get to where we want to go.

For example, successful people often demonstrate an ability to be flexible when executing their plans, learning to roll with adversity and obstacles. They also tend to be lifelong learners and have the ability to stay committed to their vision, even when things aren't necessarily going their way. Most have had to deal with failure on some level, and have even learned from their setbacks, becoming stronger and more committed as a result. Perhaps even more importantly, they are often doggedly determined to achieve their goals, to the point where giving up is not an option that they allow themselves to consider.

It's no secret that BUD/S is amongst the most intense military training programs in the entire world. For more than six months, SEAL candidates are pushed to their absolute mental and physical limits all in an effort to get them to say two words—"I quit." This is especially true during Hell Week, the grueling five-and-a-half-day "sufferfest" that is a part of Phase One.

During Hell Week, SEAL candidates can count on being tired, wet, cold, and hungry pretty much the entire time. It is the perfect environment for testing the dedication and mental toughness of an individual, with those not suited to becoming a SEAL often washing out during those grueling few days.

But those who do decide to leave BUD/S training don't simply ask their instructors if they may be excused from the program. Instead, they must signal their desire to quit by ringing a bell that is suspended on a wooden post located in a central courtyard known as "the grinder." When a trainee is ready to call it quits, he or she must walk up to the bell, clang it loudly in front of the entire class, and then place their training helmet on the ground next to the post. It is a ritual that is designed to make the act of giving up a very humiliating and public affair, forcing the person ringing the bell to take ownership of their failure at the same time.

Throughout Hell Week the instructors are constantly badgering the candidates, attempting to cajole them into giving up. They'll tell them "all you have to do is ring the bell and all of this pain and suffering will go away." They'll make it sound like a very tempting option, providing those who aren't strong enough to continue with a way to opt out. It can be hard to resist those thoughts when you're three days into Hell Week, haven't slept more than four or five hours the entire time, and are cold and wet from spending hours in the water.

"

Little minds are tamed and subdued by misfortune, but great minds rise above them."

—Washington Irving

More often than not, those who are able to survive Hell Week aren't the ones who are necessarily the strongest, fastest, or fittest. Instead, they are the individuals who are mentally strong enough to compartmentalize the pain, ignore the fatigue, and push any thoughts of quitting out of their head. In other words, they refuse to ring the bell because they know if they do it will probably be something that they'll regret for the rest of their lives. They want to avoid the "Permanent Pain of Regret" at all costs.

Taking a similar approach to pursuing our goals can lead to success in our lives as well. We all know that there will be setbacks along the way and times when we will question whether or not we're on the right path—after all, few things worth doing in life ever come easy. There will also be times when our plans will fall apart, sometimes in spectacular fashion. But by refusing to give up, we come out stronger and more prepared to achieve our objectives than we were when we first started. By refusing to ring the bell, we are committing ourselves to seeing our goals through to the end, which is often times more than half of the battle.

Tenacity is one of the most common traits of individuals who have been highly successful. Legend has it that Thomas Edison made a thousand iterations of the lightbulb before finding the one design that actually worked. Similarly, Henry Ford declared bankruptcy twice before he launched the Ford Motor Company. George Lucas saw the original *Star Wars* film turned down by United Artists, Universal, and Disney before Fox finally gave him the green light to make the film.

In each of these cases, the individuals involved could have chosen to give up on their dream and move on to other projects, but instead they refused to ring the bell on their ambitions. Ultimately this led to overwhelming success for each of them, although it didn't always seem like they were heading in the right direction at the time. But a determined person with a clear vision can achieve great things, potentially changing the world in the process.

Walt Disney is often viewed as a paragon of American success. In his lifetime, he was able to build a lucrative movie and animation studio and a massively popular theme park, both of which laid the foundations for what would become one of the largest multimedia conglomerates in the world. As a creative force, Disney was responsible for producing more than eighty movies, countless animated shorts, and hundreds of hours of television programs over the span of fifty years. Along the way, he also collected forty-eight Academy Awards, while still finding time to found the California Institute of the Arts.

With a resume like that, it's hard to argue that Disney was anything but a success, although his road to fame and fortune didn't exactly start as a smooth one. In fact, in the early days of his career, it seemed Walt was destined to be a failure with one misstep after another. At the age of twenty-two, he was forced to declare bankruptcy after a cartoon series that he pitched failed to generate much interest. He was even fired from a job drawing comics for a local newspaper in Missouri because his manager thought he wasn't creative enough.

When his early animation ambitions didn't pan out, Walt decide to head to Los Angeles, where he and his brother Roy set up the Disney Brothers Studio. One of their first big projects was producing a new animated series for Universal Pictures based on a character Walt created named Oswald the Lucky Rabbit. The cartoons were a hit, but when Disney tried to renegotiate a better contract with Universal, he learned that not only did he not own the rights to the Oswald character, but that most of his animation staff had been hired away from him as well. Universal's intention was to continue producing Oswald animated shorts on its own, cutting Walt out of the creative process altogether.

At that point, it would have been easy for Disney to call it quits. In a matter of days he had gone from the producer of a popular series of cartoons, to a man without a job. Universal had unceremoniously taken away his one and only successful project and stolen his team of artists and animators all at the same time. It was a serious blow to his fledgling company, which had only just begun to leave its mark on Hollywood.

Undaunted, however, Disney immediately began work on his next project. In fact, on the train ride home following that fateful meeting with the head of Universal Studio, he began sketching a new character. It was a mouse named Mickey, who would eventually go on to become the iconic symbol for the Walt Disney organization and one of the most recognized cartoon characters ever created.

It would be nice to be able to say "the rest is history," but Disney's struggles weren't quite over yet. Mickey Mouse would eventually become a smash hit, but it took some time before the character found an audience. Walt created two animated shorts featuring his budding new star, but they were released at a time when the movies were transitioning from silent films to talkies. Mickey's early appearances had to be redone to include sound, with Disney himself supplying the initial voice acting.

Over time the stress of having to keep his little animation studio open and producing cartoons began to wear on Disney. He believed that animated shorts could prove to be highly successful with moviegoers, but even though he was producing high-quality clips, the profits still weren't rolling in. In the late 1920s and early 1930s, the Disney Brothers Studio struggled to keep its doors open, which led to a great deal of anxiety for Walt.

Eventually the sleepless nights and frayed nerves caught up to him, so Disney and his wife Lillian decided to take a vacation so they could get away. The rest and relaxation proved to be good for Walt, who saw his creative juices start to flow once again. But while he and Lillian were on their extended sabbatical, the Great Depression hit the US and Europe, bringing on an economic slump unlike any the world had ever seen. For a time, it seemed as if the fates themselves were conspiring against Disney, keeping him from finding the level of success he had been searching for.

66

I'm a great believer in luck, and I find the harder I work the more I have of it."

—Thomas Jefferson

When he returned to Los Angeles from his vacation, Walt felt renewed and ready to get back to work. But the American economy was in shambles and most people had very little disposable income. Undaunted by this turn of events, Walt went to work on an entirely new project. He decided he wanted to focus on making a feature-length animated film, which at that point had never been done before. His vision resulted in *Snow White and the Seven Dwarfs*, which was finally released to the public in 1937.

Snow White took years to make and cost Disney more than two million dollars to produce, using nearly every cent that his Mickey Mouse shorts were generating for the studio at the time. Upon release, the film was dubbed "Disney's folly," as most thought it would be a major box office failure. Animated films were a novelty during that era and early critics thought *Snow White* was too long for its own good.

As it turns out, the film was both a critical and

financial success, playing to sold out theaters across the country and breaking box office records in the process. With the Great Depression lingering on, many people found escape from their own harsh reality by going to the movies, and Disney's animated film was the greatest escape of them all. It was unlike any other film ever made, proving that feature length animated movies could appeal to a wide audience. It would eventually be the foundation on which Walt Disney built his future success, turning his little animation studio into an entertainment powerhouse.

The release of *Snow White and the Seven Dwarfs* completely transformed Walt Disney's fortunes. The film went on to generate ten million dollars in box office revenue, which at the time was an enormous sum of money. It also earned Disney an Academy Honorary Award for "a significant screen innovation." When he collected the award on stage, Walt was given a full-sized Oscar statue, as well as seven miniature ones to go along with it.

The influx of cash to the Disney Brothers Studios meant that Walt and his team had the financial freedom and security to work on even more ambitious projects moving forward. Beyond that, however, the public's demand for animated feature films helped to buoy the flagging economy, creating jobs not only for animators, but publicists, writers, and directors as well. Even the manufacturing sector received a bump from the film as the demand for *Snow White* merchandise grew to unprecedented levels.

For Walt, the success of his first full-length animated film vindicated everything he had been working towards for the past decade and a half. Despite all of the setbacks, trials, and tribulations, he had seen his vision come to life on the screen and loved by millions of viewers. In the years that followed, he would produce more animated and live-action films, some of which were huge successes right away, while others took time to find their audience. Eventually however, the Walt Disney name became synonymous with wholesome entertainment for the entire family, creating an empire that is worth more than $225 billion today.

The story of Walt Disney's road to success can teach us a lot about our own approach to achieving our goals. One of the biggest takeaways from Disney's life has to be his unwillingness to give up on his dream, even when faced with insurmountable challenges. There were numerous times when Disney could have easily accepted failure and moved on to an easier, less stressful, line of work. Instead, he learned from his mistakes and setbacks. This ultimately allowed him to blend his creative talents, hard work, and unmatched vision in a way that opened the doors to Walt becoming one of the most successful people of the twentieth century.

"

If opportunity doesn't knock, build a door."

—Milton Berle

It isn't easy to overcome adversity and stay focused on achieving your objectives following setbacks and failures. It takes a mindset that is disciplined, resilient, and determined, all of which are qualities that a Navy SEAL needs to possess as well. Throughout his career, a SEAL will face difficult challenges, usually without the luxury of being able to simply quit when things start to get tough. Those aren't qualities that are necessarily easy to find in a person, which is why the Navy has gone to great lengths to try to understand what type of candidates will most likely be successful at BUD/S training.

In the early 2000s, with ongoing wars in Iraq and Afghanistan, each of the branches of the armed forces was ordered to increase the number of Special Forces operatives within their ranks over the course of a five year period. However, as the deadline for increasing the number of SEALs grew nearer, the Navy found itself falling well short of its projected goals. In an effort to correct this problem, a study was conducted with the goal of identifying common characteristics amongst those who successfully graduated from BUD/S. The idea being that by knowing which characteristics made someone more likely to become a SEAL, the Navy could focus on recruiting those specific types of individuals.

The study, which was released in 2010, indicated that while being a competitive athlete played a significant role in completing BUD/S, successful candidates often had a background in a few very specific sports, which weren't necessarily the ones you might expect. Conventional wisdom might lead outside observers to guess that football players would make ideal SEALs; after all those athletes are strong, fast, and have a proven track record for working within the game plan of a team. In reality, water polo was the sport that led the way, with boxing, wrestling, triathlon, swimming, rugby, and lacrosse also making the list. Rock climbers and mountain bikers also scored extremely high. If a SEAL candidate participated in any of those activities, he was twice as likely to graduate from the training program compared to those who didn't.

But that wasn't the only revealing information that was gained from the study. Researchers also found that if a candidate was a competitive athlete who also happened to play chess, he was three times more likely to make it through BUD/S. From a mental standpoint, chess players understand the value of thinking several moves ahead and visualizing potential outcomes well in advance. This seems to serve them particularly well during training, allowing them to understand the benefits of a specific exercise and how it will assist them in future endeavors, whereas non-chess players could potentially struggle to see the bigger picture.

There were other interesting things to be gleaned from the study as well. For instance, it was learned that most SEAL candidates don't actually quit while in the midst of a training session. In other words, they don't tend to give up while they're on a ten-mile run in cold and wet conditions. Instead, the majority of the individuals who end up ringing the bell do so over breakfast and lunch, which seems like an odd time to throw in the towel. As it turns out, it once again comes back to the trainees' mental toughness and outlook on potential failure.

While an individual is actually in the moment, they are much more capable of processing and understanding exactly what is happening to them, allowing them to deal with difficult conditions in a more efficient manner. When they are wet, tired, and hungry, they tend to accept the current state of affairs and just deal with the difficulties at hand, all the while looking forward to the time when their suffering is over. By knowing exactly what is expected of them, they can endure the toughest of conditions and adapt as needed, rarely looking ahead to the next challenge.

The main reason why most people actually quit over breakfast and lunch is because their brains are already processing the challenges that they'll face in an upcoming training exercise and calculating the chances for potential failure. Rather than give up in the middle of such a challenge, they decide to opt out before they even start. Their brains tell them that whatever they're about to embark on is going to be very hard and they're probably not going to make it through anyway, so they might as well quit ahead of time.

This is a trait that isn't unique to individuals who are training to become SEALs, but is actually a fairly widespread phenomenon. Many people have a self-defeating attitude when it comes to pursuing their passion projects and big goals, often telling themselves that they won't be able to achieve the things they want in life anyway, so why even try? In a sense, they are giving up before they've even attempted to put in any kind of meaningful effort.

Having confidence in your own abilities and a strong enough mindset to avoid feeling defeated before you ever leave the starting gate are essential traits for finding success. Envisioning what it is you hope to achieve is often times the first step towards that goal, but it can also be quite daunting at the same time. The trick is to not let the enormity of the task dissuade you from ever starting. Instead, break down the large, overriding goal into smaller, more digestible, micro-goals that are easier to wrap your brain around. Micro-goals tend to be less scary, making it easier to take those initial first steps towards achieving them.

For a SEAL candidate enrolled in BUD/S, there is no such thing as a typical day. The training schedule can vary greatly from one day to the next, although the focus is usually on physical training, or PT as it is referred to in the military. In the case of

BUD/S, PT usually involves long open water swims, fast-paced runs in soft sand, or performing sit-ups, push-ups, and pull-ups in the training compound. Much of that activity takes place in the shadow of that iconic bell, which seems to loom large over the proceedings.

That kind of continuous training can be both mentally and physically taxing, so trying to envision making it to the end of the week, or even a single day, can seem extremely difficult at times. But if the candidate can break each day down into segments, creating micro-goals to help get them through the various PT sessions, it becomes much easier to process. Instead of thinking that today he needs to run four miles on the beach, swim two miles in the ocean, and complete thousands of push-ups, flutter-kicks, and sit-ups, he can instead choose to tell himself that he just needs to get through the first mile of the run before turning his focus on to the second mile, then the third, and so on. Eventually, the run will be over and the candidate will move to the next phase of the training schedule, taking things one micro-goal at a time.

The same philosophy can prove useful for

achieving just about anything we set our mind to in life. Whether it's training to run a marathon, working towards getting a degree, or opening our own business, using the micro-goals approach can be an efficient and handy way to achieve the things we want. In our minds, those types of larger, macro-goals can seem nearly impossible at first, but by breaking them down into smaller steps, they become much more approachable and realistic.

Over time, as those micro-goals turn into micro-successes, the confidence that we feel and the progress we make becomes more concrete. This makes those once hard-to-reach goals seem much more attainable, providing slow but steady progress towards the finish line. With a few meaningful successes under your belt, you'll start to realize that the things you once thought were out of reach were actually within your grasp all along. You only needed to believe in yourself and have the confidence necessary to actually pursue those objectives.

"

It is hard to fail, but it is worse never to have tried to succeed."

–Theodore Roosevelt

Academy-Award winning filmmaker Woody Allen famously said, "Showing up is 80 percent of life." In other words, you can accomplish a lot just by actually getting off the couch and putting in a little effort. The problem is, many people can't seem to find the motivation, determination, or confidence to put in even the minimal amount of effort. Instead, they end up wondering why it is that they can't attain the level of success they are looking for.

There is a lot to be said for just showing up. In a sense, it means you're ready to get serious about whatever it is you're looking to achieve in life and that you've put in enough thought, time, and effort to consider it a worthwhile venture. Many people spend a great deal of time thinking about their goals, and plotting and planning ways that they can make them a reality, only to put them aside simply because they can't take the next step. Fear, uncertainty, and doubt in their own abilities prevents them from even showing up, leaving their full potential unrealized.

The most successful people in the world don't think about the things they want to do, they actually go out and *do* the things they want to do. It is easy to talk about all of the big ideas and plans that you have for yourself, provided you never actually have to try to make them a reality. Plenty of people are content to just talk a big game, but at some point truly successful men and women stop talking and start doing. The first step on this road to success is having the courage to get started.

If showing up is 80 percent of life, what does the other 20 percent consist of? That is where the hard work, discipline, and commitment come into play. While it is true that you can't really succeed at anything without first committing yourself to the project, you also won't achieve your macro-goals simply by showing up alone. Finding success requires dedication, a laser-like focus, and a willingness to sacrifice the things you want now in favor of reaching your long term goals down the line. That could mean giving up time with friends and family to focus on a personal project, spending late nights at the office rather than going home early, or cutting out your favorite foods in order to achieve some health or fitness goal. Either way, major objectives rarely come easy or without significant effort.

Elon Musk, the co-founder of Tesla, Inc., knows something about putting in a lot of hard work in order to achieve big goals. His main objective has always been to create an efficient, affordable, and technologically advanced electric vehicle for the masses, which in turn could eventually have a positive impact on the planet by reducing emissions. But as it turns out, starting a car company from scratch isn't easy and even now, more than fifteen years after Tesla was first founded, he's still having to learn new things about how cars are made.

Since its founding in 2003, Tesla has successfully launched a series of electric vehicles, redefining consumer expectations for how an EV should look and perform. First, the company produced the sporty Roadster, before following it up with a sleek-looking sedan called the Model S. Later, it would add the Model X crossover SUV, before introducing the Model 3, the first Tesla vehicle priced to reach a mass audience. But in the beginning the smaller, more affordable sedan created a host of production problems, which delayed delivery and put a dent in Tesla's normally sterling reputation. It also forced Musk to put in a considerable amount of time and effort to solve those issues.

For the most part, Tesla electric vehicles are made in a high-tech manufacturing facility called the Gigafactory 1, which is located near Reno, Nevada. When the Model 3 was first introduced, the company received more than 450,000 preorders as consumers scrambled to get their hands on the new car. That meant production needed to ramp up quickly and the Gigafactory was prepped to handle the demand. Musk promised that the production plant would be able to produce more than 20,000 vehicles per month by the end of December 2017, but when it came time to actually begin building the Model 3, Tesla's advanced facility only managed to roll out 2,425 cars over a three-month period.

Prior to the Model 3, Tesla produced luxury cars at a lower volume, enabling them to easily meet the strong, but modest, demand for the Model S and X. When it came time to start mass production on a larger scale, however, the process for going from just a few hundred vehicles a week to several thousand, proved far more challenging than anyone ever expected, Musk included.

In the early months of 2018, the assembly line at the Gigafactory continued to underperform, which led investors to begin to question Musk's leadership. Worse yet, with production slowed to a crawl, some customers canceled their Model 3 preorders, a signal that they were losing confidence as well. The new vehicle, which once looked like a major success story for Tesla, was quickly turning into a major public relations debacle.

As production issues for the Model 3 lingered on, Musk vowed to overcome the challenges that Tesla faced, boldly declaring that he would personally oversee the manufacturing process in an effort to work out the kinks in the system. It was a crucial time for the company, which was very publicly displaying the growing pains that came along with expanding into the mass market. Would Tesla be able to step up to meet demand, or would its previous successes prove to be a fluke that couldn't be repeated on a larger scale?

Overcoming the challenges of mass producing

the Model 3 would not be easy, as it required a number of tweaks—both large and small—to the Gigafactory's production line. In order to observe that process himself, Musk essentially moved into his office at the auto plant, literally staying there for days on end. Reports emerged that he was actually sleeping under his desk and putting in work weeks in excess of 120 hours, focusing all of his attention on solving Tesla's production woes.

By early summer of 2018 the Gigafactory finally started to hit its production goals, rolling out more than 5000 Model 3 cars each week. In order to get to that number, Musk and his team of engineers had to refine the assembly process, even taking the unprecedented step of removing some of the automated manufacturing robots and replacing them with human workers instead. Tesla's CEO also focused heavily on improving efficiency and raising quality control, eventually putting the company on pace to meet demand for its popular new model.

Musk's ability to work long hours has always been legendary, even before he took such a hands-on approach to getting Model 3 production up and running. But during those critical months spent solving the Gigafactory's manufacturing problems his dedication to reaching his goals became even more clear. The billionaire was so committed to his vision of an affordable electric car that he was willing to work practically nonstop for weeks at a time, which not only ate up what little free time he already had, but also had an impact on him both mentally and physically as well.

Later, when asked about the long hours he put in at Tesla, Musk is quoted as saying "There are easier places to work, but nobody changed the world on forty hours a week." Later, he would add that he believed that anyone who did want to have an impact on the planet on such a grandiose scale would need to work eighty to one hundred hours a week to accomplish their goals.

This gives us a lot of insight into Musk's motivations. Ultimately, he is looking to have a lasting impact on the planet, and he's willing to work extremely hard to achieve that goal. Tesla is a means to an end, but in order for that company to be successful, Musk himself has made, and will continue to make, the necessary sacrifices to see his vision become a reality.

"

The ultimate measure
of a man is not where
he stands in moments of
comfort and convenience,
but where he stands at
times of challenge and
controversy."

–Martin Luther King, Jr.

Our personal goals may not be quite as lofty as quite literally changing the world, but Musk's message is still clear. If you want to achieve your objectives, whether they are big or small, you're going to have to put in a lot of hard work. If you're training for a marathon, that hard work comes in the form of many miles of running in preparation for the race. If your dream is to open your own restaurant, then you'll need to put countless hours into finding the right location, renovating the space, and refining the menu. All of that takes place well before you ever open the doors to paying customers, which is when the real work actually begins.

In addition to being persistent in the pursuit of their goals and being willing to work extremely hard to achieve them, another common trait amongst successful people is an insatiable curiosity and a desire to learn new things. Whether it's keeping abreast of the latest technological innovations, studying industry trends, or immersing themselves in a new culture or language, there will always be more knowledge to be acquired. Successful people don't shy away from those challenges, but instead embrace the opportunity to expand their knowledge, adopting new ideas and thought processes that could potentially help them reach their objectives.

For these individuals, learning doesn't stop when you graduate from school, but is instead an ongoing process that continues throughout their lives. Essentially, the idea is that there will always be new things to discover and those things can play a crucial role in either your present endeavors or on future projects that you may embark upon.

Nowhere is this better demonstrated than on a SEAL team. When a SEAL candidate graduates from BUD/S and gets the chance to finally pin on the Special Warfare insignia, it is just an indication that he has learned enough to truly start learning. The educational process for a SEAL is an ongoing one that continues throughout their career. BUD/S simply provides the essential building blocks for what it takes to join the Navy's elite warriors, but to truly become good at his job, a SEAL will continue to train, hone existing skills, and learn entirely new ones throughout his time in the military and most likely beyond.

Following the successful completion of BUD/S, a SEAL will embark on eighteen months of intense pre-deployment training. At this stage of his career it is all about building the skillset necessary to serve as an efficient, reliable, and professional member of a SEAL team. During that time, he'll spend over six months in individual professional development training, six months in unit level training, and an additional six months in squad integration training. Over the course of that year and a half, the candidate will focus on learning new languages, becoming familiar with communications equipment and other technologies, and practice using an array of small arms. He'll also learn how to function as a part of a much larger unit, while improving his squad level skills and tactics, too.

A SEAL who has earned a medical rating will also attend a six-month program to become a SEAL corpsman, learning how to perform basic and advanced medical procedures in the field. Similarly, those looking to pursue a career as a SEAL officer are sent to Junior Officer Training, where they'll learn the basics of operational planning and preparation.

In total, a SEAL can spend two and a half years just in training before actually being deployed for the first time. But even after they've been assigned to a team or sent abroad, the intense training and focus on learning new things continues. This helps to keep both the mind and body sharp, which is vitally important when conducting an operation where success can hinge on split-second decision making and being as prepared as possible to take on any number of unique challenges.

Those of you who aren't Navy SEALs can still benefit from focusing on honing our skills and continually learning new things as well. Becoming a lifelong learner can have a positive impact on both your careers and personal lives, providing focus and knowledge that can help you to stay relevant in a fast-changing world. Beyond that however, studies have shown that by learning new things on a regular basis, we tend to stay healthier and happier throughout our lives too.

Many successful people are naturally very inquisitive about the world around them, which ultimately compels them to want to learn more about the things that spark their interest. But what about those of us who don't have a natural desire to obtain knowledge? How do those individuals become lifelong learners, without a healthy dose of natural curiosity as an existing part of their nature?

One of the first steps is recognizing that we probably don't know everything there is to know, even in an area that we may be considered an expert. Such is the case with a SEAL, who is already one of the finest warriors on the planet, and yet he still continues to train hard, broaden the scope of his knowledge, and look to acquire new skills that allow him to do his job better. By bringing that same sensibility to your own career or personal objectives, you're already heading in the right direction towards becoming a lifelong learner. The knowledge you gain along the way will only help to fuel your success, bringing versatility and adaptability along with it.

Another way of feeding the fire of curiosity within yourself is to adopt an apprentice-like approach to learning new things. That means seeking out those who know more about a topic than we do and absorbing some of their knowledge and expertise. By reading books, watching videos, studying websites, or interacting with an expert in person, we can glean some insights that might not have been apparent to us before.

Even SEALs take this approach when it comes to furthering their training and knowledge. While SEAL instructors are usually amongst the most knowledgeable and experienced military personnel in the Teams, they don't necessarily have all of the skills and expertise that is needed to teach the men under their watch. On occasion, the Navy will reach out to civilians who can serve as a resource to help fill the gaps in an otherwise strict and demanding training program.

"

Most people are
accustomed to a
comfortable life and so
they never go beyond
the limits. Don't be like
them."

– Usain Bolt

Recognizing that we still have a lot to learn, and taking the necessary steps to find the resources needed to improve our knowledge is not a sign of weakness. On the contrary, it is actually a significant strength to be able to identify the areas that we need to improve upon. Actively looking for ways to eliminate the deficits in our knowledge and training takes focus and discipline too, but those qualities almost always pay dividends in the end.

The list of famous people who found success after learning new things later in life is long and distinguished. Heavyweight boxer Rocky Marciano, who finished his career undefeated at 49-0, didn't even start boxing until he was in his early twenties. That may not seem very old, but for a world-class athlete, that's an advanced age to begin training for a new sport.

Similarly, famed chef Julia Child had very little exposure to gourmet cooking until she was well into her thirties. She moved to Paris with her husband in 1948—at the age of thirty-six—and began to explore her fascination with French culture and cuisine while living there. Nearly fifteen years passed before her breakout book, *Mastering the Art of French Cooking*, was published, turning Child into a media sensation who transcended the culinary world. She continued to work into her nineties, always looking to perfect some new recipe or incorporate interesting and unique ingredients into her dishes.

While probably not quite as well-known as Rocky Marciano and Julia Child, Russian adventurer Fedor Konyukhov has assembled quite an impressive resume for himself in his later years. As a young man, he was considered one of the brightest and most talented artists in the former Soviet Union, but after the Iron Curtain fell, he found great success as an explorer and mountaineer as well.

Konyukhov, who also happens to be an Eastern Orthodox priest, summited Mt. Everest in 1992, at the age of forty. Over the course of the next few years, he would go on to climb the highest peaks on the other six continents around the world, finishing the so-called Seven Summits in 1997, at a time when such a feat was still relatively rare and unusual. Later, he would go on to complete what is known as the "Explorers Grand Slam" by skiing to both the North and South Pole. At the time, he was just the third person in history to achieve that feat.

To accomplish all of that after the age of forty would be impressive in its own right, but that's just the tip of the iceberg when it comes to Konyukhov's achievements. In 2008 for example, he became the first person to make a solo circumnavigation of Antarctica in a sailboat, braving the treacherous Southern Ocean for 102 days completely alone. He was fifty-six years old at the time.

He'd follow up his successful sailing adventure with crossings of both the Atlantic and Pacific Oceans in a rowboat. After that, he would climb Everest again at the age of sixty, only to then embark on a series of long-distance dogsled expeditions that included three more visits to the North Pole. In 2016, when he was sixty-four years old, he even circled the globe in a hot air balloon. On that journey, the Russian explorer spent eleven straight days in a tiny enclosed canopy drifting high above the Earth, setting a new hot air balloon speed record in the process.

These amazing feats have made Konyukhov one of the most well-rounded and ambitious adventurers of the past century. But what really allows him to stand out amongst other explorers is the diversity of his expeditions. Not only is he an excellent high altitude mountaineer, but he is also an accomplished polar explorer, sailor, ocean rower, balloon pilot, and more. He even still manages to find time to paint and write books.

Clearly Fedor Konyukhov is a lifelong learner. For nearly three decades he has been redefining the limits of human endurance, often in completely new and unique fields of endeavor. In order to do that, he has had to continually learn new skills and expand his knowledge to the point where he practically starts all over again once he sets out in pursuit of his next objective. For Fedor, the question isn't whether or not he can achieve the things he sets his mind to, but how he can acquire the necessary skills he needs to reach those goals.

One of the other impressive things about Konyukhov is that he isn't content to simply sit back and revel in his past successes, despite the fact that they are numerous. Instead, he is continually looking ahead towards the next challenge and thinking about things that he still has left to accomplish.

Even before he completes his next grueling expedition, he is more than likely already planning what will come after that.

Once again, this is another common trait amongst successful people. Not only do they tend to consider reaching their goals a *fait accompli*, they are often juggling multiple projects at once. For them, reaching the finish line is not necessarily the end of the story, but is instead just another milestone on their way to the next goal. It isn't a manner of *if* they'll achieve their objectives, but *when*.

In this way, success is seen as a journey, not a destination, and it should be viewed as something that is ongoing. For a budding marathon runner, that means completing the first marathon is just the first phase of that journey, with the potential for future races to follow. In those future events, just finishing may no longer be the measure of success, however; improving speed and time becoming the new focus.

Achieving our goals is always a good thing, and it is important to stop and celebrate them along the way. But it is just as important to not get too comfortable either. There are always new frontiers to conquer, both within ourselves and in the world around us. There will be new challenges to overcome and new goals to pursue throughout our lifetime, and complacency can turn into the hardest obstacle to overcome of them all.

There is a saying amongst Navy SEALs: "The only easy day was yesterday." This has almost become a mantra within the Teams, pushing them to train harder, work smarter, and continually test themselves in new and unique ways. Because the moment you become complacent and content with what you've achieved is the moment when you also become irrelevant. Striving to become better in life, no matter what you do for a living or where your goals lie, can prevent this from happening and keep you on track to achieving the objectives that you've set for yourself.

When you reach that milestone moment, don't be afraid to stop and enjoy the accomplishment. After all, you've more than earned it. But don't rest on your laurels for too long, because chances are there are still other things you'd like to achieve. Don't let complacency and self-satisfaction rob you of all of the things that you have left to accomplish.

Instead, turn your attention to whatever it is that comes next.

In the end, if you truly want to know the secret to finding success, consider this: If you stay focused and disciplined, remain confident and persistent, and commit to learning new things throughout your lifetime, chances are you won't have to worry about finding success. Instead, it will almost assuredly find you.

66

The way to get started
is to quit talking and
begin doing."

–Walt Disney